HEAVY BAG
COMBINATIONS

The Ultimate Guide to Heavy Bag Punching Combinations

BOOK 2 OF A CONTINUING SERIES

SAMMY FRANCO

Also by Sammy Franco

Invincible: Mental Toughness Techniques for Peak Performance
Unleash Hell: A Step-by-Step Guide to Devastating Widow Maker Combinations
Feral Fighting: Advanced Widow Maker Fighting Techniques
The Widow Maker Program: Extreme Self-Defense for Deadly Force Situations
Stand and Deliver: A Street Warrior's Guide to Tactical Combat Stances
Maximum Damage: Hidden Secrets Behind Brutal Fighting Combinations
First Strike: End a Fight in Ten Seconds or Less!
The Bigger They Are, The Harder They Fall
Self-Defense Tips and Tricks
Kubotan Power: Quick & Simple Steps to Mastering the Kubotan Keychain
The Complete Body Opponent Bag Book
Heavy Bag Training: Boxing, Mixed Martial Arts & Self-Defense
Gun Safety: For Home Defense and Concealed Carry
Out of the Cage: A Guide to Beating a Mixed Martial Artist on the Street
Warrior Wisdom: Inspiring Ideas from the World's Greatest Warriors
Savage Street Fighting: Tactical Savagery as a Last Resort
War Machine: How to Transform Yourself Into a Vicious and Deadly Street Fighter
1001 Street Fighting Secrets
When Seconds Count: Self-Defense for the Real World
Killer Instinct: Unarmed Combat for Street Survival
Street Lethal: Unarmed Urban Combat

Heavy Bag Combinations: The Ultimate Guide to Heavy Bag Combinations
Copyright © 2015 by Sammy Franco
ISBN: 978-1-941845-15-8
Printed in the United States of America

Published by Contemporary Fighting Arts, LLC.
Visit us Online at: **www.SammyFranco.com**
Follow us on Twitter: **@RealSammyFranco**

For author interviews or publicity information, please send inquiries in care of the publisher.

Contents

"The whole is greater than the sum of its parts."

- Aristotle

Caution!

The author, publisher, and distributors of this book disclaim any liability from loss, injury, or damage, personal or otherwise, resulting from the information and procedures in this book. This book is for academic study only.

The information contained in this book is not designed to diagnose, treat, or manage any physical health conditions.

Before you begin any exercise or activity, including those suggested in this book, it is important to check with your physician to see if you have any condition that might be aggravated by strenuous training.

About this book

Heavy Bag Combinations is my second book in the Heavy Bag
Training Series. Practitioners who use this book as a reference tool
will dramatically improve their heavy bag training skills. In fact, the
punching combinations featured in this text will significantly improve
your fighting skills, enhance your fitness and conditioning, and
breathe new life into your current heavy bag workout sessions.

The heavy bag punching combinations featured in this book will
also help you achieve maximum training performance in a variety
of activities including, boxing (professional and amateur), mixed
martial arts, kickboxing, self-defense, and personal fitness.

This book also provides step-by-step instructions for performing
beginner, intermediate and advanced heavy bag combinations.
Many experienced fighters will find these punching combinations
very challenging. However, the best feature of this book is that

it teaches you how to create an unlimited number of heavy bag workout programs filled with an infinite amount of unique punching combinations.

The heavy bag techniques featured in this book are based on my 30+ years of research, training and teaching the martial arts and combat sciences. I have taught these unique punching combinations to thousands of students, and I'm confident they will help you reach higher levels of training performance.

Heavy Bag Combinations has four chapters, each one covers a critical aspect of training. This book assumes you currently possess the basic punching skills. However, for those of you who need a quick refresher course, I have provided step-by-step instructions for all of the punching techniques in the appendix of this book. In addition, you will also find a glossary of terms. Since this is both a skill-building workbook and training guide, feel free to write in the margins, underline passages, and dog-ear the pages.

Finally, I encourage you to read this book from beginning to end, chapter by chapter. Only after you have read the entire book should you treat it as a reference and skip around, reading those chapters or combinations that directly apply to you.

Train hard!

- *Sammy Franco*

Chapter 1
Beginner Combinations

Understanding Combination Punching

Since this book is devoted strictly to punching combinations, it's important for you to have a very clear understanding of its meaning. A combination or "compound attack" is the logical sequence of two or more techniques thrown in strategic succession. For example, a jab followed by a rear cross is considered to be a basic punching combination.

Unlimited Number of Combinations

Besides the actual body mechanics of punching, there are several other elements that comprise a punching combination. They include attack rhythms, height variations, the cadence of delivery, and practitioner movement. However, these are vast topics and must be reserved for future books. Nevertheless, when you combine and manipulate all of these elements you truly have an infinite amount of punching combinations that you can perform on the heavy bag.

When reading the combination sequence on the following pages, please note that the word "high" indicates punches delivered at head level while "low" represents punches delivered to the stomach level on the bag.

Once again, this book assumes you can perform the basic punching skills, including the jab, rear cross, hook and uppercut. However, if you are not familiar with these foundational punching techniques, please see the step-by-step instructions featured in the appendix of this book. Let's begin with beginner level punching combinations.

Combination #1: jab-jab (all high)

Step 1: Begin from a fighting stance.

Step 2: Extend your lead arm forward and jab the bag.

Step 3: Return to the stance position.

Step 4: Jab again at the bag.

Combination #2: jab-jab (all low)

Step 1: Begin from a fighting stance.

Step 2: Bend your knees while snapping your lead arm at the bag.

Step 3: Return to a low stance position.

Step 4: Again, bend your knees and jab low at the bag.

Combination #3: jab-jab (high-low)

Step 1: Begin from a fighting stance.

Step 2: Jab high at the bag.

Step 3: Return to a low stance position.

Step 4: Jab low at the bag.

Combination #4: jab-jab (low-high)

Step 1: Begin from a fighting stance.

Step 2: Bend your knees and jab low at the bag.

Step 3: Return to a low stance position.

Step 4: Quickly shoot up and jab high at the bag.

Combination #5: jab-rear cross (all high)

Step 1: Begin from a fighting stance.

Step 2: Jab high at the bag.

Step 3: Next, deliver a rear cross to the top of the bag.

Step 4: Return to the stance position

Combination #6: jab-rear cross (high-low)

Step 1: Begin from a fighting stance.

Step 2: Jab high at the bag.

Heavy Bag Combinations

Step 3: Next, deliver a low rear cross.

Step 4: Return to your stance.

Combination #7: rear cross-jab (all high)

Step 1: Begin from a fighting stance.

Step 2: Next, deliver a high rear cross.

Step 3: Jab high at the bag.

Step 4: Return to your stance.

Combination #8: jab-rear cross-rear cross (all high)

Step 1: Begin from a fighting stance.

Step 2: Jab high at the bag.

17

Step 3: Next, deliver a rear cross to the top of the bag.

Step 4: Return to your stance.

Step 5: Deliver another rear cross.

Step 6: Return to your stance.

Combination #9: rear cross-jab-rear cross-jab (all high)

Step 1: Start from a fighting stance.

Step 2: Deliver a rear cross to the top of the bag.

Step 3: Jab high at the bag.

Step 4:Fire off a second rear cross.

Step 5: Jab again at the bag.

Step 6: Return to the stance position.

Combination #10: jab-jab-rear cross (all high)

Step 1: Begin from a fighting stance.

Step 2: Jab high at the bag.

Step 3: Return to the stance position.

Step 4: Jab again at the bag.

Step 5: Next, follow up with a rear cross to the top of the bag.

Step 6: Return to the stance position.

Combination #11: jab-jab-rear cross (high-high-low)

Step 1: Start from a fighting stance.

Step 2: Throw a high jab at the bag.

Step 3: Return to the stance position.

Step 4: Jab again at the bag.

Heavy Bag Combinations

Step 5: Next, deliver a low rear cross at the bag.

Step 6: Return to your stance.

Combination #12: jab-rear cross-jab (all high)

Step 1: Begin from a fighting stance.

Step 2: Jab high at the bag.

Step 3: Next, deliver a rear cross to the top of the bag.

Step 4: Follow up with another high jab.

Combination #13: jab-rear cross-jab (high-low-high)

Step 1: Begin from a fighting stance.

Step 2: Jab high at the bag.

Step 3: Next, deliver a rear cross punch to the lower portion of the bag.

Step 4: Follow up with another high jab.

Combination #14: jab-rear cross-jab-rear cross (all high)

Step 1: Begin from a fighting stance.

Step 2: Jab high at the bag.

Step 3: Next, deliver a rear cross to the top of the bag.

Step 4: Follow up with another high jab.

Step 5: Deliver another high rear cross.

Step 6: Return to your stance.

Combination #15: jab-rear cross-jab-rear cross (high-low-high-low)

Step 1: Begin from a fighting stance.

Step 2: Jab high at the bag.

Step 3: Next, deliver a low rear cross.

Step 4: Throw another high jab.

Step 5: Follow up with another low rear cross.

Step 6: Return to the stance position.

Combination #16: jab-rear cross-jab-rear cross (low-high-low-high)

Step 1: Begin from a fighting stance.

Step 2: Throw a low jab to the bag.

Step 3: Next, a high rear cross.

Step 4: Follow up with another low jab.

Step 5: Finish off with a high rear cross..

Step 6: Return to the stance position.

Combination #17: jab-rear cross-jab-rear cross (all low)

Step 1: Begin from a fighting stance.

Step 2: Deliver a low jab at the bag.

Step 3: Next, a low rear cross.

Step 4: Follow up with another low jab.

Step 5: Finish off with a low rear cross.

Step 6: Return to the fighting stance.

Combination #18: jab-jab-rear cross (low-low-high)

Step 1: Begin from a fighting stance.

Step 2: Throw a low jab at the bag.

Step 3: Return to a low stance position.

Step 4: Throw another low jab.

Step 5: Follow with a rear cross to the top of the bag.

Step 6: Return to the stance position.

Combination #19: jab-jab-jab (high-low-high)

Step 1: Begin from a fighting stance.

Step 2: Jab high at the bag.

Step 3: Return to a low stance position.

Step 4: Jab low at the bag.

Step 5: Jab high at the bag.

Step 6: Return to the stance position.

Chapter 2
Intermediate Combinations

Adding Hooks to Your Combinations

In this chapter, we are going to build off the combinations from the previous chapter and add circular punches to your heavy bag workout. More specifically, you're going to add hook punches to your punching combinations.

The hook punch is a devastating blow delivered from both the lead and rear side of the body. However, it's also one of the most difficult to master. To execute the hook punch correctly, you must maintain the correct wrist, forearm, and shoulder alignment. When delivering the punch, be sure your arm is bent at least 90 degrees and that your wrist and forearm are kept straight throughout the movement.

To execute the hook punch, quickly and smoothly raise your elbow up so that your arm is parallel to the ground while simultaneously torquing your shoulder, hip, and foot in the direction of the blow. As you throw the punch, be sure that your fist is positioned vertically. Never place your fist horizontally when throwing a hook. This inferior hand placement can cause a sprained or broken wrist. Avoid chambering or cocking the arm and excessive follow-through.

If you require more information about performing the hook punch, please see the appendix of this book.

Combination #20: jab-rear cross-hook (all high)

Step 1: Begin from a fighting stance.

Step 2: Throw a high jab at the bag.

Step 3: Next, deliver a high rear cross.

Step 4: Immediately follow with a lead hook punch.

Combination #21: jab-rear cross-hook (high-high-low)

Step 1: Begin from a fighting stance.

Step 2: Extend you lead arm forward and jab the bag.

Step 3: Next, deliver a rear cross.

Step 4: Immediately follow with a low lead hook punch.

Combination #22: jab-rear cross-hook-hook (all high)

Step 1: Begin from a fighting stance.

Step 2: Extend your lead arm forward and jab the bag.

Step 3: Next, deliver a rear cross to the top of the bag.

Step 4: Immediately follow with a lead hook punch.

Step 5: Next, deliver a rear hook.

Step 6: Return to your stance.

Combination #23: jab-rear cross-hook-hook (high-high-high-low)

Step 1: Begin from a fighting stance.

Step 2: Jab the bag.

Step 3: Next, deliver a rear cross.

Step 4: Immediately follow with a lead hook.

Step 5: Next, a low rear hook.

Step 6: Return to the fighting stance.

Combination #24: jab-rear cross-hook-hook (high-high-low-high)

Step 1: Begin from a fighting stance.

Step 2: Jab the bag.

Step 3: Next, deliver a rear cross.

Step 4: Immediately follow with a low lead hook punch.

Step 5: Deliver a rear hook punch.

Step 6: Return to the stance position.

Combination #25: jab-rear hook-rear hook (high-high-low)

Step 1: Start from a fighting stance.

Step 2: Jab high at the bag.

Step 3: Next, deliver a high rear hook.

Step 4: Follow with a low rear hook.

Combination #26: jab-rear hook-rear hook (high-low-high)

Step 1: Begin from a fighting stance.

Step 2: Jab high at the bag.

Step 3: Next, deliver a low rear hook.

Step 4: Follow with a high rear hook punch.

Combination #27: jab-lead hook-rear cross (all high)

Step 1: Begin from a fighting stance.

Step 2: Jab high at the bag.

Step 3: From the same arm, deliver a high lead hook.

Step 4: Next, throw a rear cross.

Combination #28: jab-lead hook-rear cross (low-low-high)

Step 1: Begin from a fighting stance.

Step 2: Jab low at the bag.

Step 3: Next, deliver a low lead hook.

Step 4: Follow up with a rear cross.

Combination #29: jab-lead hook-rear hook (all high)

Step 1: Begin from a fighting stance.

Step 2: Jab high at the bag.

Step 3: Next, from the same arm, deliver a high lead hook.

Step 4: Follow up with a high rear hook.

Combination #30: jab-lead hook-rear cross-lead hook (all high)

Step 1: Begin from a fighting stance.

Step 2: Jab high at the bag.

Step 3: Next, from the same arm, deliver a high lead hook.

Step 4: Follow up with a rear cross.

Step 5: A high lead hook.

Step 6: Return to the stance position.

Combination #31: jab-lead hook-rear hook (high-low-low)

Step 1: Begin from a fighting stance.

Step 2: Jab high at the bag.

Step 3: Next, deliver a low lead hook.

Step 4: Follow up with a low rear hook.

Combination #32: jab-lead hook-rear hook (high-high-low)

Step 1: Begin from a fighting stance.

Step 2: Jab high at the bag.

Step 3: Next, from the same arm, deliver a high lead hook.

Step 4: Follow up with a low rear hook.

Combination #33: jab-lead hook-rear hook (high-low-high)

Step 1: Begin from a fighting stance.

Step 2: Jab high at the bag.

Step 3: Next, deliver a low lead hook.

Step 4: Follow up with a high rear hook.

Combination #34: jab-jab-rear cross-lead hook (all high)

Step 1: Begin from a fighting stance.

Step 2: Jab high at the bag.

Step 3: Quickly retract your punch.

Step 4: Follow up with another high jab.

Step 5: Next, throw a high rear cross.

Step 6: A high lead hook completes the compound attack.

Combination #35: jab-jab-rear cross-lead hook (high-high-high-low)

Step 1: Begin from a fighting stance.

Step 2: Jab high at the bag.

Step 3: Quickly retract your punch.

Step 4: Follow up with another high jab.

Step 5: Next, throw a high rear cross.

Step 6: A low lead hook completes the compound attack.

Combination #36: rear cross-lead hook-lead hook-rear hook (low-high-high-low)

Step 1: Begin from a fighting stance.

Step 2: Deliver a low rear cross at the bag.

Step 3: Next, a high lead hook.

Step 4: Quickly retract your punch.

Step 5: Throw another high lead hook at the bag.

Step 6: Finish with a low rear hook.

Combination #37: rear cross-lead hook-lead hook-rear hook (high-low-low-high)

Step 1: Begin from a fighting stance.

Step 2: Throw a high rear cross.

Step 3: Next, a low lead hook.

Step 4: Return to a low stance position.

Step 5: Deliver another low lead hook to the bag.

Step 6: Finish with a high rear hook.

Combination 38: rear cross-lead hook-rear cross-lead hook-rear hook (high-high-low-high-low)

Step 1: Begin from a fighting stance.

Step 2: Throw a high rear cross.

Step 3: Next, a high lead hook at the bag.

Step 4: Follow with a low rear cross.

Step 5: Deliver another lead hook.

Step 6: Finish with a low rear hook.

Combination 39: rear cross-rear hook-rear hook-lead hook-lead hook (high-high-low-low-low)

Step 1: Begin from a fighting stance.

Step 2: Throw a high rear cross.

Step 3: Next, a high rear hook.

Step 4: Deliver a low rear hook.

Step 5: Follow with a low lead hook to the bag.

Step 6: Return to a low stance position.

Step 7: Fire off another low lead hook.

Step 8: Return to your fighting stance.

Heavy Bag Combinations

Chapter 3
Advanced Combinations

Adding Uppercuts to Your Combinations

In this chapter, we are going to build off the combinations from the previous two chapters and add uppercuts to your heavy bag combinations. The uppercut is an explosive and powerful close-quarter punch that travels in a vertical trajectory to its target. Uppercuts can also be delivered from either your lead or rear arm.

To execute the uppercut, quickly twist and lift your body in the direction of the blow. Make sure that the punch has a short arc and that you avoid any "winding up" motions. A properly executed uppercut should feel like an explosive jolt.

Once again, if you require more information about performing the uppercut, please see the appendix of this book.

Combination #40: jab-jab-rear uppercut (all high)

Step 1: Begin from a fighting stance.

Step 2: Jab high at the bag.

Step 3: Quickly retract your punch.

Step 4: Jab again at the bag.

Step 5: Next, throw a rear uppercut.

Step 6: Return to your fighting stance.

Combination #41: jab-lead uppercut-rear cross (all high)

Step 1: Begin from a fighting stance.

Step 2: Jab high at the bag.

Step 3: Next, throw a lead uppercut.

Step 4: Follow up with a rear cross.

Combination #42: jab-lead uppercut-rear cross (low-high-low)

Step 1: Begin from a fighting stance.

Step 2: Jab low at the bag.

Step 3: Next, throw a lead uppercut.

Step 4: Finish with a low rear cross.

Combination #43: jab-rear uppercut-lead uppercut (all high)

Step 1: Begin from a fighting stance.

Step 2: Jab high at the bag.

Step 3: Next, throw a rear uppercut.

Step 4: Finish with a lead uppercut.

Combination 44: jab-rear uppercut-lead uppercut-rear cross-lead hook (all high)

Step 1: Begin from a fighting stance.

Step 2: Jab high at the bag.

Step 3: Next, throw a rear uppercut.

Step 4: Follow up with a lead uppercut.

Step 5: Deliver a high rear cross.

Step 6: Finish with a high lead hook.

Combination #45: jab-rear cross-lead hook-rear uppercut (all high)

Step 1: Begin from a fighting stance.

Step 2: Jab high at the bag.

Step 3: Next, a high lead hook.

Step 4: Finish with a rear uppercut.

Combination #46: jab-rear cross-lead hook-rear cross (all high)

Step 1: Begin from a fighting stance.

Step 2: Jab high at the bag.

Step 3: Throw a high rear cross.

Step 4: Next, a high lead hook.

Step 5: Another high rear cross.

Step 6: Return to your fighting stance.

Combination #47: jab-rear cross-lead hook-rear cross-lead hook-lead hook (5x high-1 low)

Step 1: Begin from a fighting stance.

Step 2: Jab high at the bag.

Step 3: Throw a high rear cross.

Step 4: Next, a high lead hook.

Step 5: A high rear cross.

Step 6: A high lead hook.

Step 7: A low lead hook.

Step 8: Return to your fighting stance.

Combination #48: rear cross-jab-rear hook (all high)

Step 1: Begin from a fighting stance.

Step 2: Throw a high rear cross.

Step 3: Jab high at the bag.

Step 4: Follow up with a high rear hook.

Combination #49: rear cross-jab-rear hook-lead uppercut-lead hook (high-high-low-high-high)

Step 1: Begin from a fighting stance.

Step 2: Throw a high rear cross.

Step 3: Jab high at the bag.

Step 4: Next, a low rear hook.

Step 5: Follow up with a lead uppercut.

Step 6: Finish with a high lead hook.

Combination #50: rear cross-lead hook-rear cross-lead hook-rear uppercut (high-high-high-low-high)

Step 1: Begin from a fighting stance.

Step 2: Throw a high rear cross.

133

Step 3: Next, a high lead hook.

Step 4: Another rear cross.

Step 5: A low lead hook.

Step 6: Finish with a rear uppercut.

Combination #51: rear hook-lead hook-rear hook-lead uppercut (all high)

Step 1: Begin from a fighting stance.

Step 2: Throw a high rear hook.

Step 3: Next a high lead hook.

Step 4: Follow up with a high rear hook.

Step 5: Next, a lead uppercut.

Step 6: Return to your fighting stance.

Combination #52: rear hook-lead hook-rear hook-lead hook-rear uppercut (high-low-low-low-high)

Step 1: Begin from a fighting stance.

Step 2: Throw a high rear hook.

Step 3: Next, a low lead hook.

Step 4: Follow up with a low rear hook.

Step 5: Deliver another low lead hook.

Step 6: Finish with a rear uppercut.

Combination #53: rear uppercut-lead uppercut-rear hook-lead hook (all high)

Step 1: Begin from a fighting stance.

Step 2: Throw a rear uppercut.

Step 3: Next, a lead uppercut.

Step 4: Follow with a high rear hook.

Step 5: Next, a high lead hook.

Step 6: Return to your fighting stance.

Combination #54: rear uppercut-lead uppercut-rear uppercut-lead uppercut (all high)

Step 1: Begin from a fighting stance.

Step 2: Throw a rear uppercut.

Step 3: Follow up with a lead uppercut.

Step 4: Deliver another rear uppercut.

Step 5: Throw a final lead uppercut.

Step 6: Return to a fighting stance.

Combination #55: lead uppercut-rear uppercut-lead uppercut-rear uppercut-lead hook-lead hook-rear hook

Step 1: Begin from a fighting stance.

Step 2: Throw a lead uppercut.

Step 3: Next, a rear uppercut.

Step 4: Follow up with a lead uppercut.

Step 5: A high rear hook.

Step 6: Next, a high lead hook.

Step 7: Deliver a high rear hook.

Step 8: Return to a fighting stance.

Combination #56: rear uppercut-lead hook-rear hook-lead uppercut-lead hook (all high)

Step 1: Begin from a fighting stance.

Step 2: Deliver a rear uppercut.

Step 3: Next, a high lead hook.

Step 4: Throw a high rear hook.

Step 5: Follow with a lead uppercut.

Step 6: Next, a high lead hook.

Combination #57: jab-rear cross-lead & rear hooks-lead & rear uppercuts (all high)

Step 1: Begin from a fighting stance.

Step 2: Jab high at the bag.

Step 3: Throw a high rear cross.

Step 4: Next, a high lead hook.

Step 5: Deliver a high rear hook.

Step 6: A lead uppercut.

Step 7: Follow with a rear uppercut.

Step 8: Return to your fighting stance.

Chapter 4
Creating the Ultimate Heavy Bag Workout

Time-Based Heavy Bag Training

In my first book, *Heavy Bag Training,* I discussed the importance of creating time-based heavy bag workouts. Essentially, a time-based heavy bag workout is predicated on "rounds" and it's the best way to organize your workout. Before you begin, however, you need to decide on the duration of your heavy bag rounds as well as the rest intervals.

For example, mixed martial artists, boxers and kickboxers will often hit the heavy bag for three-minute rounds and then rest for a one-minute period. Depending on their level of conditioning and specific training goals, they might do this for a total of five to eight rounds.

Initially, you'll need to experiment with both the round duration and rest intervals to see what works best for you. Remember to start off slow and progressively build up the intensity and duration of your workouts.

To get you started on the right track, I have included some sample time-based workouts you might want to try. Keep in mind, the advanced level workouts are for elite athletes who have a minimum of five years of heavy bag training.

Sample Time Based Heavy Bag Workouts			
Skill Level	Duration of Each Round	Rest Period	Total Number of rounds
Beginner	1 minute	2 minutes	3
Beginner	1 minute	1 minute	3
Beginner	2 minutes	2 minute	3
Beginner	2 minutes	1 minute	3
Intermediate	3 minutes	2 minutes	5
Intermediate	3 minutes	1 minute	5
Intermediate	3 minutes	2 minute	6
Intermediate	3 minutes	1 minute	6
Advanced	4 minutes	2 minutes	8
Advanced	4 minutes	1 minute	8
Advanced	5 minutes	2 minutes	10
Advanced	5 minutes	1 minute	10

A Word of Caution Before you Start Training!

Take your time when working out on the bag. If you are learning how to use the heavy bag for the very first time, I strongly urge you to take your time and develop the proper punching body mechanics before tearing into the bag.

Remember, the heavy bag is a serious piece of training equipment and it's easy to get injured when using it. Heavy bag workouts are also tough and very demanding on the body. Avoid premature exhaustion by pacing yourself during your workouts. Remember, it's not a race! Enjoy the process of learning how to use the bag with skill and finesse.

Warning! Before you begin any exercise program, including those suggested in this book, it is important to check with your physician to see if you have any condition that might be aggravated by strenuous exercise.

The Art of Combination Blending

All of the punching combinations featured in this book are both foundational and challenging and will keep you busy for many years to come. In fact, you can make significant progress by sticking with the basic combinations featured in each chapter and just performing them over and over again for the duration of your round.

However, for those of you who require a greater challenge in your heavy bag training, you can perform "*combination blending.*" Essentially, combination blending is strategically combining two heavy bag combinations into one seamless combination duration a training round.

For example, if you are a beginner, you would pick two combination sequences from *Chapter 1: (Beginner Combinations)* of this book. For instance, you might pick combination #3 and combination #13.

- **Combination #3: jab-jab (high-low)**
- **Combination #13: jab-rear cross-jab (high-low-high)**

Next, you would combine the two punching sequences and perform them on the heavy bag for the duration of a three minute round. The entire combination sequence would look like the following:

Combination Blending Example: Combination 3+13= jab-jab (high-low)-jab-rear cross-jab (high-low-high)

Step 1: Begin from a fighting stance.

Step 2: Jab high at the bag.

Step 3: Return to a low stance position.

Step 4: Jab low at the bag.

Step 5: Jab high at the bag.

Step 6: Next, deliver a low rear cross at the bag.

Step 7: Follow up with another high jab.

Step 8: Return to your stance.

Here is another example of combination blending. However, this time we are going to blend combinations for an advanced practitioner. Again, this requires you to pick at least two combination sequences from *Chapter 3: (Advanced Combinations)* of this book. For instance, you might pick combination #42 and combination #48.

- **Combination #42: jab-lead uppercut-rear cross (low-high-low)**
- **Combination #48: rear cross-jab-rear hook (all high)**

Next, you would combine the two sequences and perform them on the heavy bag for the duration of your round. This sequence would look like the following:

- **Combination 42+48 = jab-lead uppercut-rear cross (low-high-low)+rear cross-jab-rear hook (all high)**

Combination 42+48 = jab-lead uppercut-rear cross (low-high-low)+rear cross-jab-rear hook (all high)

Step 1: Begin from a fighting stance.

Step 2: Jab low at the bag.

Step 3: Throw a lead uppercut.

Step 4: Next, a low rear cross.

Step 5: Follow with a high rear cross.

Step 6: Deliver a high jab.

Step 7: Finish with high rear hook.

Is Combination Blending Necessary?

Some of you might be wondering if combination blending is necessary for heavy bag training? Or if some of the combination sequences are too lengthy for practical punching applications. After all, how many punches does one really need for an effective compound attack? Well, the answer to these questions really depends on the individual and their personal training goals. Nevertheless, I've included combination blending in this book for some of the following important reasons:

1. It generates a truly unlimited supply of heavy bag combinations that will literally challenge you for a lifetime.

2. It prevents your workout routines from becoming boring, stagnant, and monotonous.

3. It's a great mental toughness exercise that develops important attributes like attention control, instrumental aggression, immediate resilience, and self-confidence.

Reversing the Combination Blending Sequence

Combination blending is the most challenging form of heavy bag training. Like I stated earlier, when used correctly, you can create an infinite amount of punching combinations that will challenge you for the rest of your life!

Moreover, you can also reverse the sequence of the blended combination. For instance, the kinesthetic feel and strategic application of punching sequence 42+48 will be substantially different from 48+42. If you don't believe me, try it out on the heavy bag and see for yourself.

Combination Blending Tips

It's important not to exceed your skill level when performing combination blending. For example, if you're a beginner, never integrate advanced or intermediate combinations into your heavy bag workout. Be patient and stick to guidelines outlined in this book.

However, intermediate practitioners are encouraged to integrate beginner level combinations with combination blending. Likewise, advanced practitioners may add beginner and intermediate punching combinations with advanced combinations. Please refer to the accompanying chart for more information.

For your convenience, I have also provided several combination blending samples for beginner, intermediate, and advanced levels of training. Again, these are just examples of what you can do in your training.

Combination Blending Examples			
	Beginner level	Intermediate level	Advanced level
Sequence	1+2	20+23	40+1
Sequence	1+3	25+27	42+25
Sequence	4+8	1+28	45+8
Sequence	4+12	11+31	5+50
Sequence	5+3	12+36	51+19
Sequence	6+9	19+34	54+6
Sequence	7+13	27+39	10+55
Sequence	8+5	33+20	48+12
Sequence	9+13	21+22	57+3
Sequence	10+14	35+17	47+29
Sequence	11+8	24+30	44+13
Sequence	14+1	26+2	49+58
Sequence	12+6	37+33	55+38
Sequence	15+17	39+19	53+12
Sequence	18+5	16+26	41+41

Punching Combination Review

For your convenience, I have provided a list of all of the punching combinations featured in each of the chapters.

Chapter 1: Beginner Combinations

1. jab-jab (all high)

2. jab-jab (all low)

3. jab-jab (high-low)

4. jab-jab (low-high)

5. jab-rear cross (all high)

6. jab-rear cross (high-low)

7. rear cross-jab (all high)

8. jab-rear cross-rear cross (all high)

9. rear cross-jab-rear cross-jab (all high)

10. jab-jab-rear cross (all high)

11. jab-jab-rear cross (high-high-low)

12. jab-rear cross-jab (all high)

13. jab-rear cross-jab (high-low-high)

14. jab-rear cross-jab-rear cross (all high)

15. jab-rear cross-jab-rear cross (high-low-high-low)

16. jab-rear cross-jab-rear cross (low-high-low-high)

17. jab-rear cross-jab-rear cross (all low)

18. jab-jab-rear cross (low-low-high)

19. jab-jab-jab (high-low-high)

Chapter 2: Intermediate Combinations

20. jab-rear cross-hook (all high)

21. jab-rear cross-hook (high-high-low)

22. jab-rear cross-hook-hook (all high)

23. jab-rear cross-hook-hook (high-high-high-low)

24. jab-rear cross-hook-hook (high-high-low-high)

25. jab-rear hook-rear hook (high-high-low)

26. jab-rear hook-rear hook (high-low-high)

27. jab-lead hook-rear cross (all high)

28. jab-lead hook-rear cross (low-low-high)

29. jab-lead hook-rear hook (all high)

30. jab-lead hook-rear cross-lead hook (all high)

31. jab-lead hook-rear hook (high-low-low)

32. jab-lead hook-rear hook (high-high-low)

33. jab-lead hook-rear hook (high-low-high)

34. jab-jab-rear cross-lead hook (all high)

35. jab-jab-rear cross-lead hook (high-high-high-low)

36. rear cross-lead hook-lead hook-rear hook (low-high-high-low)

37. rear cross-lead hook-lead hook-rear hook (high-low-low-high)

38. rear cross-lead hook-rear cross-lead hook-rear hook (high-high-low-high-low)

39. rear cross-rear hook-rear hook-lead hook-lead hook (high-high-low-low-low)

Chapter 3: Advanced Combinations

40. jab-jab-rear uppercut (all high)

41. jab-lead uppercut-rear cross (all high)

42. jab-lead uppercut-rear cross (low-high-low)

43. jab-rear uppercut-lead uppercut (all high)

44. jab-rear uppercut-lead uppercut-rear cross-lead hook (all high)

45. jab-rear cross-lead hook-rear uppercut (all high)

46. jab-rear cross-lead hook-rear cross (all high)

47. jab-rear cross-lead hook-rear cross-lead hook-lead hook (5x high-1 low)

48. rear cross-jab-rear hook (all high)

49. rear cross-jab-rear hook-lead uppercut-lead hook (high-high-low-high-high)

50. rear cross-lead hook-rear cross-lead hook-rear uppercut (high-high-high-low-high)

51. rear hook-lead hook-rear hook-lead uppercut (all high)

52. rear hook-lead hook-rear hook-lead hook-rear uppercut (high-low-low-low-high)

53. rear uppercut-lead uppercut-rear hook-lead hook (all high)

54. rear uppercut-lead uppercut-rear uppercut-lead uppercut (all high)

55. lead uppercut-rear uppercut-lead uppercut-rear uppercut-lead hook-lead hook-rear hook

56. rear uppercut-lead hook-rear hook-lead uppercut-lead hook (all high)

57. jab-rear cross-lead & rear hooks-lead & rear uppercuts (all high)

Create Your Own Punching Combinations

To get you into the creative process of developing punching combinations, I have provided a section for you to write down your own heavy bag combinations.

1.

2.

3.

4.

5.

6.

7.

8.

9.

10.

11.

12.

13.

14.

15.

16.

17.

18.

Heavy Bag Combinations

19.

20.

21.

22.

23.

24.

25.

26.

27.

28.

29.

30.

31.

32.

33.

34.

35.

36.

37.

38.

39.

40.

You Need to Move Around the Bag

To ensure that you would clearly understand all of the principles featured in this book, I intentionally had every punching technique photographed from a stationary position.

However, when working out on the heavy bag, you should always move around. This concept is important for some of the following important reasons:

1. It increases the overall intensity of your heavy bag workout.

2. It amplifies the power of your punches.

3. It gives you a greater understanding and appreciation of fighting ranges.

4. It develops good fighting habits. For example, it makes you a more elusive target when fighting an actual opponent.

The following series of photographs demonstrate how to move around the heavy bag when throwing a series of punches.

Step 1: Begin with a high jab.

Step 2: Jab again as you move clockwise around the bag.

Step 3: Throw a high rear hook at the bag.

Step 4: As the bag swings, move clockwise again.

Step 5: Jab again.

Step 6: Jab low at the bag.

Step 7: Continue to move clockwise around the bag.

Step 8: Jab high at the bag.

Step 9: Follow with a rear cross.

Step 10: Throw a lead hook.

Step 11: Next, a rear hook punch.

Step 12: Follow with a low lead hook.

Step 13: Continue to move clockwise and jab at the bag.

Step 14: Next, throw a high rear hook.

Step 15: Jab low at the bag.

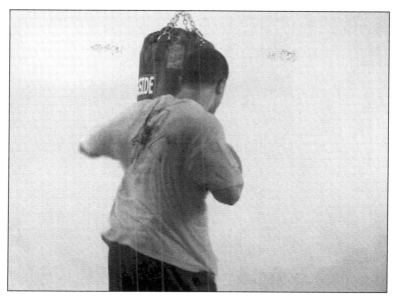

Step 16: Follow up with a lead hook.

Step 17: As you complete a circle around the heavy bag, deliver one final jab.

NOTES

_____

_____

_____

_____

_____

_____

_____

_____

_____

_____

_____

_____

_____

_____

_____

_____

Heavy Bag Resources

Heavy Bag Videos

If you wish to explore additional information about heavy bag training, I encourage you to check out the following video and book resources. Instructional videos include the following:

- *Heavy Bag Training*
- *Punching Bag Combinations*

Both videos are available for purchase on my website and amazon.com

Heavy Bag Training DVD

Punching Bag Combinations DVD

Heavy Bag Books

You can also find the entire heavy bag training book series at amazon.com. They are available in both paperback and kindle editions.

Heavy Bag Training
Book #1

Heavy Bag Routines
Book #3

Appendix

Foundational Heavy Bag Skills

In this section, I am going to teach you the foundational punching techniques required to perform all of the heavy bag combinations featured in this book. These basic skills include the fighting stance, mobility and footwork, jab, rear cross, hooks and uppercuts. Let's begin with the fighting stance..

The Fighting Stance

The fighting stance defines your ability to execute both offensive and defensive techniques, and it will play a material role in the outcome of a combat situation. It stresses strategic soundness and simplicity over complexity and style. The fighting stance also facilitates optimum execution of your body weapons while simultaneously protecting your vital targets against quick counter strikes.

The fighting stance is designed around the centerline. The centerline is an imaginary vertical line running through the center of the body, from the top of your head to the bottom of the groin. Most of your vital targets are situated along this line, including the head, throat, solar plexus, and groin. Obviously, you want to avoid directly exposing your centerline to the assailant. To achieve this, position your

Pictured here, a left lead fighting stance.

feet and body at a 45-degree angle from the opponent. This moves your body targets back and away from direct strikes but leaves you strategically positioned to attack.

When assuming a fighting stance, place your strongest and most coordinated side forward. For example, a right-handed person stands with his or her right side toward the assailant. Keeping your strongest side forward enhances the speed, power, and accuracy of your strike. This doesn't mean that you should never practice fighting from your other side. You must be capable of fighting from both sides, and you should spend equal practice time on the left and right stances.

Many people make the costly mistake of stepping forward to assume a fighting stance. Do not do this! This action only moves you closer to your assailant before your protective structure is soundly established. Moving closer to your assailant also dramatically reduces your defensive reaction time. So get into the habit of stepping backward to assume your stance. Practice this daily until it becomes a natural and economical movement.

How to Assume a Fighting Stance

When assuming your fighting stance, place your feet about shoulder width apart. Keep your knees bent and flexible. Think of your legs as power springs to launch you through the ranges of unarmed combat (kicking, punching, and grappling range).

Mobility is also important, as we'll discuss later. All footwork and strategic movement should be performed on the balls of your feet. Your weight distribution is also an important factor. Since combat is dynamic, your weight distribution will frequently change. However, when stationary, keep 50 percent of your body weight on each leg and always be in control of it.

The hands are aligned one behind the other along your centerline. The lead arm is held high and bent at approximately 90 degrees. The rear arm is kept back by the chin. Arranged this way, the hands not only protect the upper centerline but also allow quick deployment of your body weapons. When holding your guard, do not tighten your shoulder or arm muscles prior to striking. Stay relaxed and loose. Finally, keep your chin slightly angled down. This diminishes target size and reduces the likelihood of a paralyzing blow to your chin or a lethal strike to your throat.

The best method for practicing your fighting stance is in front of a full-length mirror. Place the mirror in an area that allows sufficient room for movement; a garage or basement is perfect. Stand in front of the mirror, far enough away to see your entire body. Stand naturally with your arms relaxed at your sides. Now close your eyes and quickly assume your fighting stance. Open your eyes and check for flaws. Look for low hand guards, improper foot positioning or body angle, rigid shoulders and knees, etc. Drill this way repeatedly, working from both the right and left side. Practice this until your fighting stance becomes second nature.

Footwork & Mobility

Next are footwork and mobility. I define mobility as the ability to move your body quickly and freely, which is accomplished through basic footwork. The safest footwork involves quick, economical steps performed on the balls of your feet, while you remain relaxed and balanced. Keep in mind that balance is your most important consideration.

Basic footwork can be used for both offensive and defensive purposes, and it is structured around four general directions: forward, backward, right, and left. However, always remember this footwork rule of thumb: Always move the foot closest to the direction you want to go first, and let the other foot follow an equal distance. This prevents cross-stepping, which can cost you your life in a high-risk combat situation.

Basic Footwork Movements

1. Moving forward (advance)- from your fighting stance, first move your front foot forward (approximately 12 inches) and then move your rear foot an equal distance.

2. Moving backward (retreat) - from your fighting stance, first move your rear foot backward (approximately 12 inches) and then move your front foot an equal distance.

3. Moving right (sidestep right) - from your fighting stance, first move your right foot to the right (approximately 12 inches) and then move your left foot an equal distance.

4. Moving left (sidestep left) - from your fighting stance, first move your left foot to the left (approximately 12 inches) and then move your right foot an equal distance.

Practice these four movements for 10 to 15 minutes a day in front of a full-length mirror. In a couple weeks, your footwork should be quick, balanced, and natural.

Circling Right and Left

Strategic circling is an advanced form of footwork where you will use your front leg as a pivot point. This type of movement can also be used defensively to evade an overwhelming assault or to strike the opponent from various strategic angles. Strategic circling can be performed from either a left or right stance.

Circling left (from a left stance) - this means you'll be moving your body around the opponent in a clockwise direction. From a left stance, step 8 to 12 inches to the left with your left foot, then use your left leg as a pivot point and wheel your entire rear leg to the left until the correct stance and positioning is acquired.

Circling right (from a right stance) - from a right stance, step 8 to 12 inches to the right with your right foot, then use your right leg as a pivot point and wheel your entire rear leg to the right until the correct stance and positioning is acquired.

Punching Techniques

In this section, I'm going to teach you four different punching skills that you will be using during you heavy bag workouts. They are:

- **Jab**
- **Rear cross (aka Straight Right)**
- **Hook punch**
- **Uppercut punch**

The Jab

The jab is a linear punch thrown from your lead arm, and contact is made with the center knuckle. To execute the technique, perform the following steps.

1. Start off in a fighting stance with both of your hands held up in the guard position. Your fists should be lightly clenched with both of your elbows pointing to the ground.

2. Simultaneously step toward the opponent and twist your front waist and shoulder forward as you snap your front arm into the target.

3. When delivering the punch, remember not to lock out your arm as this will have a "pushing effect" on the target.

4. Quickly retract your arm back to the starting position.

5. One common mistake when throwing the punch is to let it deflect off to the side of the target. Also, keep in mind that jabs can be delivered to the opponent's head or body. Targets

for the punch include the opponent's nose, chin, and solar plexus.

Pictured here, the jab.

Rear Cross or Straight Right

The rear cross is considered the heavy artillery of punches and it's thrown from your rear arm. To execute the punch, perform the following steps:

1. Start off in a fighting stance with both of your hands held up in the guard position. Your fists should be lightly clenched with both of your elbows pointing to the ground.

2. Next, quickly twist your rear hips and shoulders forward as you snap your rear arm into the target. Proper waist twisting and weight transfer is of paramount importance to the rear cross. You must shift your weight from your rear foot to your lead leg as you throw the punch.

3. To maximize the impact of the punch, make certain that your fist is positioned horizontally. Avoid overextending the blow or exposing your chin during its execution.

4. Once again, do not lock out your arm when throwing the punch. Let the power of the blow sink into the target before you retract it back to the starting position.

The rear cross.

Hook Punch

The hook is another devastating punch in your arsenal, yet it's also one of the most difficult to master. This punch can be performed from either your front or rear hand, and it can be delivered to both high or low targets.

1. Start in a fighting stance with your hand guard held up. Both of your elbows should be pointing to the ground, and your fists clenched loosely.

2. Next, quickly and smoothly, raise your elbow up so that your

arm is parallel to the ground while simultaneously torquing your shoulder, hip, and foot into the direction of the blow.

3. When delivering the strike, be certain your arm is bent at least ninety degrees and that your wrist and forearm are kept straight throughout the movement.

4. As you throw the punch, your fist is positioned vertically. The elbow should be locked when contact is made with the target. Remember to simultaneously tighten your fists when impact is made with the target. This action will allow your punch to travel with optimum speed and efficiency, and it will also augment the impact power of your strike.

5. Return to the starting position.

The lead hook punch.

Uppercut Punch

The uppercut is a another powerful punch that can be delivered from both the lead and rear arm. To execute the blow, perform the following steps.

1. Start off in a fighting stance with both of your hands held up in the guard position. Your fists should be lightly clenched with both of your elbows pointing to the ground.

2. Next, drop your shoulder and bend your knees.

3. Quickly, stand up and drive your fist upward and into the target. Your palm should be facing you when contact is made with the target. To avoid any possible injury, always keep your wrists straight.

4. Make certain your punch has a tight arc. Avoid "winding up" the blow. A properly executed uppercut punch should be a tight explosive jolt.

5. Return to the fighting stance.

The rear uppercut.

The lead uppercut punch.

Heavy Bag Combinations

Glossary

A

accuracy—The precise or exact projection of force. Accuracy is also defined as the ability to execute a combative movement with precision and exactness.

adaptability—The ability to physically and psychologically adjust to new or different conditions or circumstances of combat.

advanced first-strike tools—Offensive techniques that are specifically used when confronted with multiple opponents.

aerobic exercise—Literally, "with air." Exercise that elevates the heart rate to a training level for a prolonged period of time, usually 30 minutes.

affective preparedness – One of the three components of preparedness. Affective preparedness means being emotionally, philosophically, and spiritually prepared for the strains of combat. See cognitive preparedness and psychomotor preparedness.

aggression—Hostile and injurious behavior directed toward a person.

aggressive response—One of the three possible counters when assaulted by a grab, choke, or hold from a standing position. Aggressive response requires you to counter the enemy with destructive blows and strikes. See moderate response and passive response.

aggressive hand positioning—Placement of hands so as to imply aggressive or hostile intentions.

agility—An attribute of combat. One's ability to move his or her body quickly and gracefully.

amalgamation—A scientific process of uniting or merging.

ambidextrous—The ability to perform with equal facility on both the right and left sides of the body.

anabolic steroids – synthetic chemical compounds that resemble the male sex hormone testosterone. This performance-enhancing drug is known to increase lean muscle mass, strength, and endurance.

analysis and integration—One of the five elements of CFA's mental component. This is the painstaking process of breaking down various elements, concepts, sciences, and disciplines into their atomic parts, and then methodically and strategically analyzing, experimenting, and drastically modifying the information so that it fulfills three combative requirements: efficiency, effectiveness, and safety. Only then is it finally integrated into the CFA system.

anatomical striking targets—The various anatomical body targets that can be struck and which are especially vulnerable to potential harm. They include: the eyes, temple, nose, chin, back of neck, front of neck, solar plexus, ribs, groin, thighs, knees, shins, and instep.

anchoring – The strategic process of trapping the assailant's neck or limb in order to control the range of engagement during razing.

assailant—A person who threatens or attacks another person.

assault—The threat or willful attempt to inflict injury upon the person of another.

assault and battery—The unlawful touching of another person without justification.

assessment—The process of rapidly gathering, analyzing, and accurately evaluating information in terms of threat and danger. You can assess people, places, actions, and objects.

attack—Offensive action designed to physically control, injure, or kill another person.

attitude—One of the three factors that determine who wins a street fight. Attitude means being emotionally, philosophically, and spiritually liberated from societal and religious mores. See skills and knowledge.

attributes of combat—The physical, mental, and spiritual qualities that enhance combat skills and tactics.

awareness—Perception or knowledge of people, places, actions, and objects. (In CFA, there are three categories of tactical awareness: criminal awareness, situational awareness, and self-awareness.)

B

balance—One's ability to maintain equilibrium while stationary or moving.

blading the body—Strategically positioning your body at a 45-degree angle.

blitz and disengage—A style of sparring whereby a fighter moves into a range of combat, unleashes a strategic compound attack, and then quickly disengages to a safe distance. Of all sparring methodologies, the blitz and disengage most closely resembles a real street fight.

block—A defensive tool designed to intercept the assailant's attack by placing a non-vital target between the assailant's strike and your vital body target.

body composition—The ratio of fat to lean body tissue.

body language—Nonverbal communication through posture, gestures, and facial expressions.

body mechanics—Technically precise body movement during the execution of a body weapon, defensive technique, or other fighting maneuver.

body tackle – A tackle that occurs when your opponent haphazardly rushes forward and plows his body into yours.

body weapon—Also known as a tool, one of the various body parts that can be used to strike or otherwise injure or kill a criminal assailant.

burn out—A negative emotional state acquired by physically over- training. Some symptoms include: illness, boredom, anxiety, disinterest in training, and general sluggishness.

C

cadence—Coordinating tempo and rhythm to establish a timing pattern of movement.

cardiorespiratory conditioning—The component of physical fitness that deals with the heart, lungs, and circulatory system.

centerline—An imaginary vertical line that divides your body in half and which contains many of your vital anatomical targets.

choke holds—Holds that impair the flow of blood or oxygen to the brain.

circular movements—Movements that follow the direction of a curve.

close-quarter combat—One of the three ranges of knife and bludgeon combat. At this distance, you can strike, slash, or stab your assailant with a variety of close-quarter techniques.

cognitive development—One of the five elements of CFA's mental component. The process of developing and enhancing your fighting skills through specific mental exercises and techniques. See analysis and integration, killer instinct, philosophy, and strategic/tactical development.

cognitive exercises—Various mental exercises used to enhance fighting skills and tactics.

cognitive preparedness – One of the three components of preparedness. Cognitive preparedness means being equipped with the strategic concepts, principles, and general knowledge of combat. See affective preparedness and psychomotor preparedness.

combat-oriented training—Training that is specifically related to the harsh realities of both armed and unarmed combat. See ritual-oriented training and sport-oriented training.

combative arts—The various arts of war. See martial arts.

combative attributes—See attributes of combat.

combative fitness—A state characterized by cardiorespiratory and muscular/skeletal conditioning, as well as proper body composition.

combative mentality—Also known as the killer instinct, this is a combative state of mind necessary for fighting. See killer instinct.

combat ranges—The various ranges of unarmed combat.

combative utility—The quality of condition of being combatively useful.

combination(s)—See compound attack.

common peroneal nerve—A pressure point area located approximately four to six inches above the knee on the midline of the outside of the thigh.

composure—A combative attribute. Composure is a quiet and focused mind-set that enables you to acquire your combative agenda.

compound attack—One of the five conventional methods of attack. Two or more body weapons launched in strategic succession whereby the fighter overwhelms his assailant with a flurry of full speed, full-force blows.

conditioning training—A CFA training methodology requiring the practitioner to deliver a variety of offensive and defensive combinations for a 4-minute period. See proficiency training and street training.

contact evasion—Physically moving or manipulating your body to avoid being tackled by the adversary.

Contemporary Fighting Arts—A modern martial art and self-defense system made up of three parts: physical, mental, and spiritual.

conventional ground-fighting tools—Specific ground-fighting techniques designed to control, restrain, and temporarily incapacitate your adversary. Some conventional ground fighting tactics include: submission holds, locks, certain choking techniques, and specific striking techniques.

coordination—A physical attribute characterized by the ability to perform a technique or movement with efficiency, balance, and accuracy.

counterattack—Offensive action made to counter an assailant's initial attack.

courage—A combative attribute. The state of mind and spirit that enables a fighter to face danger and vicissitudes with confidence, resolution, and bravery.

creatine monohydrate—A tasteless and odorless white powder that mimics some of the effects of anabolic steroids. Creatine is a safe body-building product that can benefit anyone who wants to increase their strength, endurance, and lean muscle mass.

criminal awareness—One of the three categories of CFA awareness. It involves a general understanding and knowledge of the nature and dynamics of a criminal's motivations, mentalities, methods, and capabilities to perpetrate violent crime. See situational awareness and self-awareness.

criminal justice—The study of criminal law and the procedures associated with its enforcement.

criminology—The scientific study of crime and criminals.

cross-stepping—The process of crossing one foot in front of or behind the other when moving.

crushing tactics—Nuclear grappling-range techniques designed to crush the assailant's anatomical targets.

cue word - a unique word or personal statement that helps focus your attention on the execution of a skill, instead of its outcome.

D

deadly force—Weapons or techniques that may result in unconsciousness, permanent disfigurement, or death.

deception—A combative attribute. A stratagem whereby you delude your assailant.

decisiveness—A combative attribute. The ability to follow a tactical course of action that is unwavering and focused.

defense—The ability to strategically thwart an assailant's attack (armed or unarmed).

defensive flow—A progression of continuous defensive responses.

defensive mentality—A defensive mind-set.

defensive reaction time—The elapsed time between an assailant's physical attack and your defensive response to that attack. See offensive reaction time.

demeanor—A person's outward behavior. One of the essential factors to consider when assessing a threatening individual.

diet—A lifestyle of healthy eating.

disingenuous vocalization—The strategic and deceptive

utilization of words to successfully launch a preemptive strike at your adversary.

distancing—The ability to quickly understand spatial relationships and how they relate to combat.

distractionary tactics—Various verbal and physical tactics designed to distract your adversary.

double-end bag—A small leather ball hung from the ceiling and anchored to the floor with bungee cord. It helps develop striking accuracy, speed, timing, eye-hand coordination, footwork and overall defensive skills.

double-leg takedown—A takedown that occurs when your opponent shoots for both of your legs to force you to the ground.

E

ectomorph—One of the three somatotypes. A body type characterized by a high degree of slenderness, angularity, and fragility. See endomorph and mesomorph.

effectiveness—One of the three criteria for a CFA body weapon, technique, tactic, or maneuver. It means the ability to produce a desired effect. See efficiency and safety.

efficiency—One of the three criteria for a CFA body weapon, technique, tactic, or maneuver. It means the ability to reach an objective quickly and economically. See effectiveness and safety.

emotionless—A combative attribute. Being temporarily devoid of human feeling.

endomorph—One of the three somatotypes. A body type characterized by a high degree of roundness, softness, and body fat. See ectomorph and mesomorph.

evasion—A defensive maneuver that allows you to strategically maneuver your body away from the assailant's strike.

evasive sidestepping—Evasive footwork where the practitioner moves to either the right or left side.

evasiveness—A combative attribute. The ability to avoid threat or danger.

excessive force—An amount of force that exceeds the need for a particular event and is unjustified in the eyes of the law.

experimentation—The painstaking process of testing a combative hypothesis or theory.

explosiveness—A combative attribute that is characterized by a sudden outburst of violent energy.

F

fear—A strong and unpleasant emotion caused by the anticipation or awareness of threat or danger. There are three stages of fear in order of intensity: fright, panic, and terror. See fright, panic, and terror.

feeder—A skilled technician who manipulates the focus mitts.

femoral nerve—A pressure point area located approximately 6 inches above the knee on the inside of the thigh.

fighting stance—Any one of the stances used in CFA's system. A strategic posture you can assume when face-to-face with an unarmed assailant(s). The fighting stance is generally used after you have launched your first-strike tool.

fight-or-flight syndrome—A response of the sympathetic nervous system to a fearful and threatening situation, during which it prepares your body to either fight or flee from the perceived danger.

finesse—A combative attribute. The ability to skillfully execute a movement or a series of movements with grace and refinement.

first strike—Proactive force used to interrupt the initial stages of an assault before it becomes a self-defense situation.

first-strike principle—A CFA principle that states that when physical danger is imminent and you have no other tactical option but to fight back, you should strike first, strike fast, and strike with authority and keep the pressure on.

first-strike stance—One of the stances used in CFA's system. A strategic posture used prior to initiating a first strike.

first-strike tools—Specific offensive tools designed to initiate a preemptive strike against your adversary.

fisted blows – Hand blows delivered with a clenched fist.

five tactical options – The five strategic responses you can make in a self-defense situation, listed in order of increasing level of resistance: comply, escape, de-escalate, assert, and fight back.

flexibility—The muscles' ability to move through maximum natural ranges. See muscular/skeletal conditioning.

focus mitts—Durable leather hand mitts used to develop and sharpen offensive and defensive skills.

footwork—Quick, economical steps performed on the balls of the feet while you are relaxed, alert, and balanced. Footwork is structured around four general movements: forward, backward, right, and left.

fractal tool—Offensive or defensive tools that can be used in more than one combat range.

fright—The first stage of fear; quick and sudden fear. See panic and terror.

full Beat – One of the four beat classifications in the Widow Maker Program. The full beat strike has a complete initiation and retraction phase.

G

going postal - a slang term referring to a person who suddenly and unexpectedly attacks you with an explosive and frenzied flurry of blows. Also known as postal attack.

grappling range—One of the three ranges of unarmed combat. Grappling range is the closest distance of unarmed combat from which you can employ a wide variety of close-quarter tools and techniques. The grappling range of unarmed combat is also divided into two planes: vertical (standing) and horizontal (ground fighting). See kicking range and punching range.

grappling-range tools—The various body tools and techniques that are employed in the grappling range of unarmed combat, including head butts; biting, tearing, clawing, crushing, and gouging tactics; foot stomps, horizontal, vertical, and diagonal elbow strikes, vertical and diagonal knee strikes, chokes, strangles, joint locks, and holds. See punching range tools and kicking range tools.

ground fighting—Also known as the horizontal grappling plane, this is fighting that takes place on the ground.

guard—Also known as the hand guard, this refers to a fighter's hand positioning.

guard position—Also known as leg guard or scissors hold, this is a ground-fighting position in which a fighter is on his back holding his opponent between his legs.

H

half beat – One of the four beat classifications in the Widow Maker Program. The half beat strike is delivered through the retraction phase of the proceeding strike.

hand positioning—See guard.

hand wraps—Long strips of cotton that are wrapped around the hands and wrists for greater protection.

haymaker—A wild and telegraphed swing of the arms executed by an unskilled fighter.

head-hunter—A fighter who primarily attacks the head.

heavy bag—A large cylindrical bag used to develop kicking, punching, or striking power.

high-line kick—One of the two different classifications of a kick. A kick that is directed to targets above an assailant's waist level. See low-line kick.

hip fusing—A full-contact drill that teaches a fighter to "stand his ground" and overcome the fear of exchanging blows with a stronger opponent. This exercise is performed by connecting two fighters with a 3-foot chain, forcing them to fight in the punching range of unarmed combat.

histrionics—The field of theatrics or acting.

hook kick—A circular kick that can be delivered in both kicking and punching ranges.

hook punch—A circular punch that can be delivered in both the punching and grappling ranges.

I

impact power—Destructive force generated by mass and velocity.

impact training—A training exercise that develops pain tolerance.

incapacitate—To disable an assailant by rendering him unconscious or damaging his bones, joints, or organs.

initiative—Making the first offensive move in combat.

inside position—The area between the opponent's arms, where he has the greatest amount of control.

intent—One of the essential factors to consider when assessing a threatening individual. The assailant's purpose or motive. See demeanor, positioning, range, and weapon capability.

intuition—The innate ability to know or sense something without the use of rational thought.

J

jersey Pull – Strategically pulling the assailant's shirt or jacket over his head as he disengages from the clinch position.

joint lock—A grappling-range technique that immobilizes the assailant's joint.

K

kick—A sudden, forceful strike with the foot.

kicking range—One of the three ranges of unarmed combat. Kicking range is the furthest distance of unarmed combat wherein you use your legs to strike an assailant. See grappling range and punching range.

kicking-range tools—The various body weapons employed in the kicking range of unarmed combat, including side kicks, push kicks, hook kicks, and vertical kicks.

killer instinct—A cold, primal mentality that surges to your consciousness and turns you into a vicious fighter.

kinesics—The study of nonlinguistic body movement communications. (For example, eye movement, shrugs, or facial gestures.)

kinesiology—The study of principles and mechanics of human movement.

kinesthetic perception—The ability to accurately feel your body during the execution of a particular movement.

knowledge—One of the three factors that determine who will win a street fight. Knowledge means knowing and understanding how to fight. See skills and attitude.

L

lead side -The side of the body that faces an assailant.

leg guard—See guard position.

linear movement—Movements that follow the path of a straight line.

low-maintenance tool—Offensive and defensive tools that require the least amount of training and practice to maintain proficiency. Low maintenance tools generally do not require preliminary stretching.

low-line kick—One of the two different classifications of a kick. A kick that is directed to targets below the assailant's waist level. (See high-line kick.)

lock—See joint lock.

M

maneuver—To manipulate into a strategically desired position.

MAP—An acronym that stands for moderate, aggressive, passive. MAP provides the practitioner with three possible responses to various grabs, chokes, and holds that occur from a standing position. See aggressive response, moderate response, and passive response.

Marathon des Sables (MdS) - a six-day, 156-mile ultramarathon held in southern Morocco, in the Sahara Desert. It is considered by many to be the toughest footrace on earth.

martial arts—The "arts of war."

masking—The process of concealing your true feelings from your opponent by manipulating and managing your body language.

mechanics—(See body mechanics.)

mental toughness - a performance mechanism utilizing a collection of mental attributes that allow a person to cope, perform and prevail through the stress of extreme adversity.

mental component—One of the three vital components of the CFA system. The mental component includes the cerebral aspects of fighting including the killer instinct, strategic and tactical development, analysis and integration, philosophy, and cognitive development. See physical component and spiritual component.

mesomorph—One of the three somatotypes. A body type classified by a high degree of muscularity and strength. The mesomorph possesses the ideal physique for unarmed combat. See ectomorph and endomorph.

mobility—A combative attribute. The ability to move your body quickly and freely while balanced. See footwork.

moderate response—One of the three possible counters when assaulted by a grab, choke, or hold from a standing position. Moderate response requires you to counter your opponent with a control and restraint (submission hold). See aggressive response and passive response.

modern martial art—A pragmatic combat art that has evolved to meet the demands and characteristics of the present time.

mounted position—A dominant ground-fighting position where a fighter straddles his opponent.

muscular endurance—The muscles' ability to perform the same

motion or task repeatedly for a prolonged period of time.

muscular flexibility—The muscles' ability to move through maximum natural ranges.

muscular strength—The maximum force that can be exerted by a particular muscle or muscle group against resistance.

muscular/skeletal conditioning—An element of physical fitness that entails muscular strength, endurance, and flexibility.

N

naked choke—A throat choke executed from the chest to back position. This secure choke is executed with two hands and it can be performed while standing, kneeling, and ground fighting with the opponent.

neck crush – A powerful pain compliance technique used when the adversary buries his head in your chest to avoid being razed.

neutralize—See incapacitate.

neutral zone—The distance outside the kicking range at which neither the practitioner nor the assailant can touch the other.

nonaggressive physiology—Strategic body language used prior to initiating a first strike.

nontelegraphic movement—Body mechanics or movements that do not inform an assailant of your intentions.

nuclear ground-fighting tools—Specific grappling range tools designed to inflict immediate and irreversible damage. Nuclear tools and tactics include biting tactics, tearing tactics, crushing tactics, continuous choking tactics, gouging techniques, raking tactics, and all striking techniques.

O

offense—The armed and unarmed means and methods of attacking a criminal assailant.

offensive flow—Continuous offensive movements (kicks, blows, and strikes) with unbroken continuity that ultimately neutralize or terminate the opponent. See compound attack.

offensive reaction time—The elapsed time between target selection and target impaction.

one-mindedness—A state of deep concentration wherein you are free from all distractions (internal and external).

ostrich defense—One of the biggest mistakes one can make when defending against an opponent. This is when the practitioner looks away from that which he fears (punches, kicks, and strikes). His mentality is, "If I can't see it, it can't hurt me."

P

pain tolerance—Your ability to physically and psychologically withstand pain.

panic—The second stage of fear; overpowering fear. See fright and terror.

parry—A defensive technique: a quick, forceful slap that redirects an assailant's linear attack. There are two types of parries: horizontal and vertical.

passive response—One of the three possible counters when assaulted by a grab, choke, or hold from a standing position. Passive response requires you to nullify the assault without injuring your adversary. See aggressive response and moderate response.

patience—A combative attribute. The ability to endure and tolerate difficulty.

perception—Interpretation of vital information acquired from your senses when faced with a potentially threatening situation.

philosophical resolution—The act of analyzing and answering various questions concerning the use of violence in defense of yourself and others.

philosophy—One of the five aspects of CFA's mental component. A deep state of introspection whereby you methodically resolve critical questions concerning the use of force in defense of yourself or others.

physical attributes—The numerous physical qualities that enhance your combative skills and abilities.

physical component—One of the three vital components of the CFA system. The physical component includes the physical aspects of fighting, such as physical fitness, weapon/technique mastery, and combative attributes. See mental component and spiritual component.

physical conditioning—See combative fitness.

physical fitness—See combative fitness.

positional asphyxia—The arrangement, placement, or positioning of your opponent's body in such a way as to interrupt your breathing and cause unconsciousness or possibly death.

positioning—The spatial relationship of the assailant to the assailed person in terms of target exposure, escape, angle of attack, and various other strategic considerations.

postal attack - see going postal.

power—A physical attribute of armed and unarmed combat. The amount of force you can generate when striking an anatomical target.

power generators—Specific points on your body that generate impact power. There are three anatomical power generators: shoulders, hips, and feet.

precision—See accuracy.

preemptive strike—See first strike.

premise—An axiom, concept, rule, or any other valid reason to modify or go beyond that which has been established.

preparedness—A state of being ready for combat. There are three components of preparedness: affective preparedness, cognitive preparedness, and psychomotor preparedness.

probable reaction dynamics - The opponent's anticipated or predicted movements or actions during both armed and unarmed combat.

proficiency training—A CFA training methodology requiring the practitioner to execute a specific body weapon, technique, maneuver, or tactic over and over for a prescribed number of repetitions. See conditioning training and street training.

proxemics—The study of the nature and effect of man's personal space.

proximity—The ability to maintain a strategically safe distance from a threatening individual.

pseudospeciation—A combative attribute. The tendency to assign subhuman and inferior qualities to a threatening assailant.

psychological conditioning—The process of conditioning the mind for the horrors and rigors of real combat.

psychomotor preparedness—One of the three components of preparedness. Psychomotor preparedness means possessing all of the physical skills and attributes necessary to defeat a formidable adversary. See affective preparedness and cognitive preparedness.

punch—A quick, forceful strike of the fists.

punching range—One of the three ranges of unarmed combat. Punching range is the mid range of unarmed combat from which the fighter uses his hands to strike his assailant. See kicking range and grappling range.

punching-range tools—The various body weapons that are employed in the punching range of unarmed combat, including finger jabs, palm-heel strikes, rear cross, knife-hand strikes, horizontal and shovel hooks, uppercuts, and hammer-fist strikes. See grappling-range tools and kicking-range tools.

Q

qualities of combat—See attributes of combat.

quarter beat - One of the four beat classifications of the Widow Maker Program. Quarter beat strikes never break contact with the assailant's face. Quarter beat strikes are primarily responsible for creating the psychological panic and trauma when Razing.

R

range—The spatial relationship between a fighter and a threatening assailant.

range deficiency—The inability to effectively fight and defend in all ranges of combat (armed and unarmed).

range manipulation—A combative attribute. The strategic manipulation of combat ranges.

range proficiency—A combative attribute. The ability to effectively fight and defend in all ranges of combat (armed and unarmed).

ranges of engagement—See combat ranges.

ranges of unarmed combat—The three distances (kicking range, punching range, and grappling range) a fighter might physically engage with an assailant while involved in unarmed combat.

raze – To level, demolish or obliterate.

razer – One who performs the Razing methodology.

razing – The second phase of the Widow Maker Program. A series of vicious close quarter techniques designed to physically and psychologically extirpate a criminal attacker.

razing amplifier - a technique, tactic or procedure that magnifies the destructiveness of your razing technique.

reaction dynamics—see probable reaction dynamics.

reaction time—The elapsed time between a stimulus and the response to that particular stimulus. See offensive reaction time and defensive reaction time.

rear cross—A straight punch delivered from the rear hand that crosses from right to left (if in a left stance) or left to right (if in a right stance).

rear side—The side of the body furthest from the assailant. See lead side.

reasonable force—That degree of force which is not excessive for a particular event and which is appropriate in protecting yourself or others.

refinement—The strategic and methodical process of improving or perfecting.

relocation principle—Also known as relocating, this is a street-fighting tactic that requires you to immediately move to a new location (usually by flanking your adversary) after delivering a compound attack.

repetition—Performing a single movement, exercise, strike, or action continuously for a specific period.

research—A scientific investigation or inquiry.

rhythm—Movements characterized by the natural ebb and flow of related elements.

ritual-oriented training—Formalized training that is conducted without intrinsic purpose. See combat-oriented training and sport-oriented training.

S

safety—One of the three criteria for a CFA body weapon, technique, maneuver, or tactic. It means that the tool, technique, maneuver or tactic provides the least amount of danger and risk for the practitioner. See efficiency and effectiveness.

scissors hold—See guard position.

scorching – Quickly and inconspicuously applying oleoresin capsicum (hot pepper extract) on your fingertips and then razing your adversary.

self-awareness—One of the three categories of CFA awareness. Knowing and understanding yourself. This includes aspects of yourself which may provoke criminal violence and which will promote a proper and strong reaction to an attack. See criminal awareness and situational awareness.

self-confidence—Having trust and faith in yourself.

self-enlightenment—The state of knowing your capabilities, limitations, character traits, feelings, general attributes, and motivations. See self-awareness.

set—A term used to describe a grouping of repetitions.

shadow fighting—A CFA training exercise used to develop and refine your tools, techniques, and attributes of armed and unarmed combat.

sharking – A counter attack technique that is used when your adversary grabs your razing hand.

shielding wedge - a defensive maneuver used to counter an unarmed postal attack.

situational awareness—One of the three categories of CFA awareness. A state of being totally alert to your immediate surroundings, including people, places, objects, and actions. (See criminal awareness and self-awareness.)

skeletal alignment—The proper alignment or arrangement of your body. Skeletal alignment maximizes the structural integrity of striking tools.

skills—One of the three factors that determine who will win a street fight. Skills refers to psychomotor proficiency with the tools and techniques of combat. See Attitude and Knowledge.

slipping—A defensive maneuver that permits you to avoid an assailant's linear blow without stepping out of range. Slipping can be accomplished by quickly snapping the head and upper torso sideways (right or left) to avoid the blow.

snap back—A defensive maneuver that permits you to avoid an assailant's linear and circular blows without stepping out of range. The snap back can be accomplished by quickly snapping the head backward to avoid the assailant's blow.

somatotypes—A method of classifying human body types or builds into three different categories: endomorph, mesomorph, and ectomorph. See endomorph, mesomorph, and ectomorph.

sparring—A training exercise where two or more fighters fight each other while wearing protective equipment.

speed—A physical attribute of armed and unarmed combat. The rate or a measure of the rapid rate of motion.

spiritual component—One of the three vital components of the CFA system. The spiritual component includes the metaphysical issues and aspects of existence. See physical component and mental component.

sport-oriented training—Training that is geared for competition and governed by a set of rules. See combat-oriented training and ritual-oriented training.

sprawling—A grappling technique used to counter a double- or single-leg takedown.

square off—To be face-to-face with a hostile or threatening assailant who is about to attack you.

stance—One of the many strategic postures you assume prior to or during armed or unarmed combat.

stick fighting—Fighting that takes place with either one or two sticks.

strategic positioning—Tactically positioning yourself to either escape, move behind a barrier, or use a makeshift weapon.

strategic/tactical development—One of the five elements of CFA's mental component.

strategy—A carefully planned method of achieving your goal of engaging an assailant under advantageous conditions.

street fight—A spontaneous and violent confrontation between two or more individuals wherein no rules apply.

street fighter—An unorthodox combatant who has no formal training. His combative skills and tactics are usually developed in the street by the process of trial and error.

street training—A CFA training methodology requiring the practitioner to deliver explosive compound attacks for 10 to 20 seconds. See condition ng training and proficiency training.

strength training—The process of developing muscular strength through systematic application of progressive resistance.

stress - physiological and psychological arousal caused by a stressor.

stressors - any activity, situation, circumstance, event, experience, or condition that causes a person to experience both physiological and psychological stress.

striking art—A combat art that relies predominantly on striking techniques to neutralize or terminate a criminal attacker.

striking shield—A rectangular shield constructed of foam and vinyl used to develop power in your kicks, punches, and strikes.

striking tool—A natural body weapon that impacts with the assailant's anatomical target.

strong side—The strongest and most coordinated side of your body.

structure—A definite and organized pattern.

style—The distinct manner in which a fighter executes or performs his combat skills.

stylistic integration—The purposeful and scientific collection of tools and techniques from various disciplines, which are strategically integrated and dramatically altered to meet three essential criteria: efficiency, effectiveness, and combative safety.

submission holds—Also known as control and restraint techniques, many of these locks and holds create sufficient pain to cause the adversary to submit.

system—The unification of principles, philosophies, rules, strategies, methodologies, tools, and techniques of a particular method of combat.

T

tactic—The skill of using the available means to achieve an end.

target awareness—A combative attribute that encompasses five strategic principles: target orientation, target recognition, target selection, target impaction, and target exploitation.

target exploitation—A combative attribute. The strategic maximization of your assailant's reaction dynamics during a fight. Target exploitation can be applied in both armed and unarmed encounters.

target impaction—The successful striking of the appropriate anatomical target.

target orientation—A combative attribute. Having a workable knowledge of the assailant's anatomical targets.

target recognition—The ability to immediately recognize appropriate anatomical targets during an emergency self-defense situation.

target selection—The process of mentally selecting the appropriate anatomical target for your self-defense situation. This is predicated on certain factors, including proper force response, assailant's positioning, and range.

target stare—A form of telegraphing in which you stare at the anatomical target you intend to strike.

target zones—The three areas in which an assailant's anatomical targets are located. (See zone one, zone two and zone three.)

technique—A systematic procedure by which a task is accomplished.

telegraphic cognizance—A combative attribute. The ability to recognize both verbal and non-verbal signs of aggression or assault.

telegraphing—Unintentionally making your intentions known to your adversary.

tempo—The speed or rate at which you speak.

terminate—To kill.

terror—The third stage of fear; defined as overpowering fear. See fright and panic.

timing—A physical and mental attribute of armed and unarmed combat. Your ability to execute a movement at the optimum moment.

tone—The overall quality or character of your voice.

tool—See body weapon.

traditional martial arts—Any martial art that fails to evolve and change to meet the demands and characteristics of its present environment.

traditional style/system—See traditional martial arts.

training drills—The various exercises and drills aimed at perfecting combat skills, attributes, and tactics.

trap and tuck – A counter move technique used when the adversary attempts to raze you during your quarter beat assault.

U

unified mind—A mind free and clear of distractions and focused on the combative situation.

use of force response—A combative attribute. Selecting the appropriate level of force for a particular emergency self-defense situation.

V

viciousness—A combative attribute. The propensity to be extremely violent and destructive often characterized by intense savagery.

violence—The intentional utilization of physical force to coerce, injure, cripple, or kill.

visualization—Also known as mental visualization or mental imagery. The purposeful formation of mental images and scenarios in the mind's eye.

W

warm-up—A series of mild exercises, stretches, and movements designed to prepare you for more intense exercise.

weak side—The weaker and more uncoordinated side of your body.

weapon and technique mastery—A component of CFA's physical component. The kinesthetic and psychomotor development of a weapon or combative technique.

weapon capability—An assailant's ability to use and attack with a particular weapon.

webbing - The first phase of the Widow Maker Program. Webbing is a two hand strike delivered to the assailant's chin. It is called Webbing because your hands resemble a large web that wraps around the enemy's face.

widow maker - One who makes widows by destroying husbands.

widow maker program - A CFA combat program specifically designed to teach the law abiding citizen how to use extreme force when faced with immediate threat of unlawful deadly criminal attack. The Widow Maker program is divided into two phases or methodologies: Webbing and Razing.

Y

yell—A loud and aggressive scream or shout used for various strategic reasons.

Z

zero beat – One of the four beat classifications of the Widow Maker, Feral Fighting and Savage Street Fighting Programs. Zero beat strikes are full pressure techniques applied to a specific target until it completely ruptures. They include gouging, crushing, biting, and choking techniques.

zone one—Anatomical targets related to your senses, including the eyes, temple, nose, chin, and back of neck.

zone three—Anatomical targets related to your mobility, including thighs, knees, shins, and instep.

zone two—Anatomical targets related to your breathing, including front of neck, solar plexus, ribs, and groin.

Photo Credits

Page 105: *Andre Ward begins his bag-work routine during a workout on Oct. 19 in Laurel. In preparation for his fight, Ward went for six, four-minute rounds with the bag during his daily training. (Photo by Jen Rynda) Permission granted.*

About Sammy Franco

With over 30 years of experience, Sammy Franco is one of the world's foremost authorities on armed and unarmed self-defense. Highly regarded as a leading innovator in combat sciences, Mr. Franco was one of the premier pioneers in the field of "reality-based" self-defense and combat instruction.

Sammy Franco is perhaps best known as the founder and creator of Contemporary Fighting Arts (CFA), a state-of-the-art offensive-based combat system that is specifically designed for real-world self-defense. CFA is a sophisticated and practical system of self-defense, designed specifically to provide efficient and effective methods to avoid, defuse, confront, and neutralize both armed and unarmed attackers.

Sammy Franco has frequently been featured in martial art magazines, newspapers, and appeared on numerous radio and television programs. Mr. Franco has also authored numerous books, magazine articles, and editorials and has developed a popular library of instructional videos.

Sammy Franco's experience and credibility in the combat science is unequaled. One of his many accomplishments in this field includes the fact that he has earned the ranking of a Law Enforcement Master Instructor, and has designed, implemented, and taught officer survival training to the United States Border Patrol (USBP). He has instructed members of the US Secret Service, Military Special Forces,

Washington DC Police Department, Montgomery County, Maryland Deputy Sheriffs, and the US Library of Congress Police. Sammy Franco is also a member of the prestigious International Law Enforcement Educators and Trainers Association (ILEETA) as well as the American Society of Law Enforcement Trainers (ASLET) and he is listed in the "Who's Who Director of Law Enforcement Instructors."

Sammy Franco is also a nationally certified Law Enforcement Instructor in the following curricula: PR-24 Side-Handle Baton, Police Arrest and Control Procedures, Police Personal Weapons Tactics, Police Power Handcuffing Methods, Police Oleoresin Capsicum Aerosol Training (OCAT), Police Weapon Retention and Disarming Methods, Police Edged Weapon Countermeasures and "Use of Force" Assessment and Response Methods.

Mr. Franco regularly conducts dynamic and enlightening seminars on different aspects of combat training, mental toughness and achieving personal peak performance.

On a personal level, Sammy Franco is an animal lover, who will go to great lengths to assist and rescue animals. Throughout the years, he's rescued everything from turkey vultures to goats. However, his most treasured moments are always spent with his beloved German Shepherd dogs.

For more information about Mr. Franco, you can visit his website at **SammyFranco.com** or follow him on Twitter **@RealSammyFranco**

Other Books by Sammy Franco

HEAVY BAG TRAINING
Boxing -Mixed Martial Arts -Self-Defense
by Sammy Franco

The heavy bag is one of the oldest and most recognizable pieces of training equipment. It's used by boxers, mixed martial artists, self-defense practitioners, and fitness enthusiasts. Unfortunately, most people don't know how to use the heavy bag correctly. Heavy Bag Training teaches you everything you ever wanted to know about working out on the heavy bag. In this one-of-a-kind book, world-renowned self-defense expert Sammy Franco provides you with the knowledge, skills, and attitude necessary to maximize the training benefits of the bag 8.5 x 5.5, paperback, photos, illus, 166 pages.

THE COMPLETE BODY OPPONENT BAG BOOK
by Sammy Franco

In this one-of-a-kind book, Sammy Franco teaches you the many hidden training features of the body opponent bag that will improve your fighting skills and boost your conditioning. With detailed photographs, step-by-step instructions, and dozens of unique workout routines, The Complete Body Opponent Bag Book is the authoritative resource for mastering this lifelike punching bag. It covers stances, punching, kicking, grappling techniques, mobility and footwork, targets, fighting ranges, training gear, time based workouts, punching and kicking combinations, weapons training, grappling drills, ground fighting, and dozens of workouts. 8.5 x 5.5, paperback, 139 photos, illustrations, 206 pages.

INVINCIBLE
Mental Toughness Techniques for Peak Performance
by Sammy Franco

Invincible is a treasure trove of battle-tested techniques and strategies for improving mental toughness in all aspects of life. It teaches you how to unlock the true power of your mind and achieve success in sports, fitness, high-risk professions, self-defense, and other peak performance activities. However, you don't have to be an athlete or warrior to benefit from this unique mental toughness book. In fact, the mental skills featured in this indispensable program can be used by anyone who wants to reach their full potential in life. 8.5 x 5.5, paperback, photos, illus, 250 pages.

236

THE WIDOW MAKER PROGRAM
Extreme Self-Defense for Deadly Force Situations
by Sammy Franco

The Widow Maker Program is a shocking and revolutionary fighting style designed to unleash extreme force when faced with the immediate threat of an unlawful deadly criminal attack. In this unique book, self-defense innovator Sammy Franco teaches you his brutal and unorthodox combat style that is virtually indefensible and utterly devastating. With over 250 photographs and detailed step-by-step instructions, The Widow Maker Program teaches you Franco's surreptitious Webbing and Razing techniques. When combined, these two fighting methods create an unstoppable force capable of destroying the toughest adversary. 8.5 x 5.5, paperback, photos, illus, 218 pages.

FERAL FIGHTING
Advanced Widow Maker Fighting Techniques
by Sammy Franco

In this sequel, Sammy Franco marches forward with cutting-edge concepts and techniques that will take your self-defense skills to entirely new levels of combat performance. Feral Fighting includes Franco's revolutionary Shielding Wedge technique. When used correctly, it transforms you into an unstoppable human meat grinder, capable of destroying any criminal adversary. Feral Fighting also teaches you the cunning art or Scorching. Learn how to convert your fingertips into burning torches that generate over 2 million scoville heat units causing excruciating pain and temporarily blindness. 8.5 x 5.5, paperback, photos, illustrations, 204 pages.

MAXIMUM DAMAGE
Hidden Secrets Behind Brutal Fighting Combination
by Sammy Franco

Maximum Damage teaches you the quickest ways to beat your opponent in the street by exploiting his physical and psychological reactions in a fight. Learn how to stay two steps ahead of your adversary by knowing exactly how he will react to your strikes before they are delivered. In this unique book, reality based self-defense expert Sammy Franco reveals his unique Probable Reaction Dynamic (PRD) fighting method. Probable reaction dynamics are both a scientific and comprehensive offensive strategy based on the positional theory of combat. Regardless of your style of fighting, PRD training will help you overpower your opponent by seamlessly integrating your strikes into brutal fighting combinations that are fast, ferocious and final! 8.5 x 5.5, paperback, 240 photos, illustrations, 238 pages.

SAVAGE STREET FIGHTING
Tactical Savagery as a Last Resort
by Sammy Franco

In this revolutionary book, Sammy Franco reveals the science behind his most primal street fighting method. Savage Street Fighting is a brutal self-defense system specifically designed to teach the law-abiding citizen how to use "Tactical Savagery" when faced with the immediate threat of an unlawful deadly criminal attack. Savage Street Fighting is systematically engineered to protect you when there are no other self-defense options left! With over 300 photographs and detailed step-by-step instructions, Savage Street Fighting is a must-have book for anyone concerned about real world self-defense. Now is the time to learn how to unleash your inner beast! 8.5 x 5.5, paperback, 317 photos, illustrations, 232 pages.

FIRST STRIKE
End a Fight in Ten Seconds or Less!
by Sammy Franco

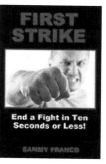

Learn how to stop any attack before it starts by mastering the art of the preemptive strike. First Strike gives you an easy-to-learn yet highly effective self-defense game plan for handling violent close-quarter combat encounters. First Strike will teach you instinctive, practical and realistic self-defense techniques that will drop any criminal attacker to the floor with one punishing blow. By reading this book and by practicing, you will learn the hard-hitting skills necessary to execute a punishing first strike and ultimately prevail in a self-defense situation. And that's what it is all about: winning in as little time as possible. 8.5 x 5.5, paperback, photos, illustrations, 202 pages.

WAR MACHINE
How to Transform Yourself Into A Vicious & Deadly Street Fighter
by Sammy Franco

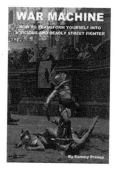

War Machine is a book that will change you for the rest of your life! When followed accordingly, War Machine will forge your mind, body and spirit into iron. Once armed with the mental and physical attributes of the War Machine, you will become a strong and confident warrior that can handle just about anything that life may throw your way. In essence, War Machine is a way of life. Powerful, intense, and hard. 11 x 8.5, paperback, photos, illustrations, 210 pages.

238

KUBOTAN POWER
Quick and Simple Steps to Mastering the Kubotan Keychain
by Sammy Franco

With over 290 photographs and step-by-step instructions, Kubotan Power is the authoritative resource for mastering this devastating self-defense weapon. In this one-of-a-kind book, world-renowned self-defense expert, Sammy Franco takes thirty years of real-world teaching experience and gives you quick, easy and practical kubotan techniques that can be used by civilians, law enforcement personnel, or military professionals. The Kubotan is an incredible self-defense weapon that has helped thousands of people effectively defend themselves. Men, women, law enforcement officers, military, and security professionals alike, appreciate this small and discreet self-defense tool. Unfortunately, however, very little has been written about the kubotan, leaving it shrouded in both mystery and ignorance. As a result, most people don't know how to unleash the full power of this unique personal defense weapon. 8.5 x 5.5, paperback, 290 photos, illustrations, 204 pages.

CONTEMPORARY FIGHTING ARTS, LLC
"Real World Self-Defense Since 1989"
www.SammyFranco.com

32611060R00141

Printed in Poland
by Amazon Fulfillment
Poland Sp. z o.o., Wrocław